ROSETREE

ROSETREE

by Sabra Loomis

Alice James Books
Cambridge, Massachusetts

ACKNOWLEDGMENTS

I would like to thank the editors of the following journals
where some of these poems first appeared:
*The American Voice, The Milkweed Chronicle, The Cincinnati Poetry
Review, Black Mountain II Review, Negative Capability, Violet,
Heaven Bone, Ark, The Manhattan Poetry Review, Raspberry Press,
The Minetta Review.*

Cover design and art by Gwen Frankfeldt based on
manuscript detail from the Roman de la Rose,
property of the Pierpont Morgan Library, New York.
Book design by Anna M. Pulaski.
Typesetting by The Writer's Center, Bethesda, Maryland.
Printed by Wickersham Printing Company, Inc.,
Lancaster, Pennsylvania.

Library of Congress Cataloging-in-Publication Data
I. Rosetree
PS3562. 0594R67 1989
811'.54 - - dc 19   88-31561
                          CIP
ISBN 0-914086-85-5

Publication of this book was made possible with support
from the Massachusetts Council on the Arts and
Humanities, a state agency whose funds are recommended
by the Governor and appropriated by the State Legislature.

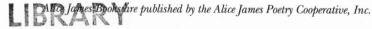

Alice James Books are published by the Alice James Poetry Cooperative, Inc.

Alice James Books
33 Richdale Avenue
Cambridge, MA 02140

For John Lamont

Contents

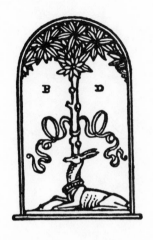

THE ROSE

The Rose

I will begin the rose,
curving inwardly with windows,
supported by tall vaults, and shadows
of the night.   I will be in the rose,
and it will be in me.   I will begin it.

So many star-rooms
collide and whisper,
partly revealed as in a dream —
the balconies softly rounded as a future.

Night descends,
past antechambers, burial rooms,
invisible vaults; on a quest
past red, past double red into azure.

Banqueting-hall doors open
into the room of night —
entered from above, into a night of roses.

There, surrounded by leaves,
protected by green hedgerows,
Creation hums and whispers,
blue in the transparent shadows.

A Window

Children stand, lit by storm-green shutters,
by the waters of memory.   Half-leaning out of windows,
they see signals in the grass, in the ivy of the garden,
the dark anterooms before the rain.

The children are coming to themselves
before the rain shutters them inside, before it
lashes the dark islands of the believers —
the zinnias and roses and anemones,
the sunflowers standing in a row.

If the children are left to themselves,
they will be lit by the letters of memory
shining upwards, they will be let into the windows
within shadows, they will stand quietly as the rain.
The children are alone, they are coming to themselves now,
before the rain, quietly, in a window.

Nightfall

A flute played in the arbor at nightfall
absolutely out into the darkness;
slow calling and fluttering and weaving there
at the shadowpoint of time, in the evening's embrace.

Wandering and falling back to earth
it spoke of greenness and of decay;
alive with whispering, with noises of a garden
and the arbor's still absorption at nightfall.

What was to become of us?
The roses spoke of so many things;
fluttering and calling us out into the dark,
into the absence at the back of the house.

Wandering and softly falling backward —
absolute melody, leaping and wavering like fire.
Then afterwards, with quietly learned steps,
with self-listening, the darkness drew backward,
beyond stillness of trees, beyond shadows of a house.

Departure

I tell of silks, of the scented air
as they cross and recross the rose-courts.
The rooms divide and merge again
in the amblings of the wind,
but the space is left entire.

I could browse within,
and still be myself, the stranger
to whom departures are given;

who feels the sea-wind darken in a room,
the coastline level, the seas rise and fall.
There is night, there is day, this is all
he knows.   He could browse forever
and still be within the red rooms.

The Window of Day

Let it breathe with the variety of springtime:
with turtle and bullfrog, lilies of the valley,
the crocus like w's in illumined script.

Let the outline rise like a tree
to hold banners, the travels of the saints
when wind took them on their journey;

and carried them to its many small islands —
past leaded cliff, down inlet and bay
to the islands across the water.

Let the outline breathe like a star.
Let it be still as a tree
to hold the upturned gaze of the mariners,
ancestors in the branches, and the sleeping children,
the musicians who play on among the fan-shaped leaves.

The Rose within Time

The rose is a moon-flower,
tossed on the darkness.   It races against clouds
born on the horizon, out of the rose of darkness,
but as clouds move and are gone, the rose will again enter
the still halls, the rooms of its welcome.

In the homecoming there is rustling above
and below, as new presences come into being,
and stand open-faced in the quiet rooms.
Others gather behind, the way children gather
in the cool dusk behind doors, to look at strangers.

There are many newcomers,
others known before, but as if in mirrors,
as if foreshadowing and gone long before.
There is a homecoming to new rooms.

The rose, long-shadowed.
If we welcome its presence within time,
there will be a passageway for the beings to go directly
into the sunlight.   If the rose remains outside,
there will be no passageway,
no cool doors, no whisperings.

Spirits of the Rose

They stand at the top of stairs and seem to meditate —
full of the night, full of the light that is within the rose,
cool and orbed and many-layered.

There is a soundlessness in their bodies,
there is the power of waiting.

The light of the rose — it is in their eyes —
in the music of hands — the urgency —
the winged light — the orbed lids —

They begin to tell the long, difficult words
of their journey: indifferent hours, the wait
in the grey darkness of tired rooms.

In a sequence unknown to us
they appear — spirits held upright —
in narrow rows — in robes of crimson —
through the long frames and spaces of the night.

In the Beginning

All was in the doing; a tumbling-out of words,
some a journey, some not even listening.

Words taught us peace with each new containment,
each discovered night.   They taught us not to stay too long.

A tumbling-out of phrases, plans, fears —
sometimes terrible in the excess, the living-out of it!
Each was a rose-word, turned inward, gathering strength.
And it still may happen that we do not build our house on earth;
it still may happen, we will not add our strength to others.

So many hours wasted
in living-outside-of-the-world.
At invisible depths, we knew —
but did not receive — the futures calling Red!   Red!

Overnight,
words gathered to become a scaffolding,
or they listened in doorways.   It was the new day:
they taught us to go slowly, and invent new meaning —
to move invisibly outward again, into the light.

TREEHOUSE EPICS:
Poems of Childhood

The House

1.

Evenings led up over the walk
to the side-door of our house.
Blue evenings ajar.

A door wide as a horse-collar
led into the calmness of cellars,
the kitchens with a slow
ticking of oilcloth.

Ladies made of moonstones
turned into anthems.
Ladies made of brooms
and a thin, gold crucifix.

2.

The house was my treehouse.
It had windows, muffled doors.
So hearty, so halo the light
from its strong chimneys.

Something moved there at night.
Something swam under the darkness,
through the shoehorn dressing-rooms —
the house had many creepers!

In the kitchen,
wind hummed through each crevice.
The teakettle moaned
with a polishing voice.

The house was my
weaver of memories.
It sang to me, out of the
hidden wood of dreams.

Rosetree, calling
with persistent voice:
Goodbye, cold wind,
I am leaving!

Green

The houses slept like orchids, unfolded like letters,
lifting their contents over the green wave.
The children slept and played in that forest —
a moss lake where bells bloomed under carpets.
In the corridor, steps waited to be gone.
The days were great listeners.

I would crawl in under rhododendrons
beside the house, into a green island of shade.
The milkman's cart, the flowerman's cart
came rumbling by, through a morning like crewelwork:
ships passing by on the horizon,
the hedges laid out, the lawns laid out;
breadcrumbs glistened on the walks for the birds.

At ten o'clock my grandfather came down the walk,
raising his hat to the passers-by.   He was on his way
to the barbershop, for a haircut or shoeshine.
The barber rolled down his wide green awning,
went in to gossip with the customers.

We found bats under our awnings
when we rolled them down each morning,
perched there like upside-down aviators,
or zealots, eyes tightly closed in prayer;
waiting for night to send its signals
over the green lawns and houses
with their closed, settled-down daylight look —
the shuttered look of survivors.

The Newspaper

Each morning the newspaper was lying at our door,
a cool dose of the world administered at sunup.
My grandfather drank his dark, bitter prune juice,
unfolded his paper and meditated on the world:
where men cheated, lied and left for South America;
people suffered migraines, sleepless nights,
amnesia and gallstones;
where children listened to conversations,
had convulsions and were bitten by snakes.

The newspaper almost covered him,
like the folded-out sheet at the barbershop,
where I looked in at him, through a low front window.

The customers stayed put in their chairs,
chins pointed frostily at the ceiling;
like mariners who had charted deep seas,
found a destination and began to freeze there, slowly.

Indians

I used to think the Indians would come down
from their gold frame above the landing,
where they hunted buffalo across the Great Plains.
They would step softly through the varnished hallway,
past a parade of mirrors, the glass-doored bookcase
with its volumes of Cooper and Ulysses S. Grant;
or drop on their heels from the twin maples on the lawn,
their faces creased and striped with paint.
They could make trails that circled like a drunk man,
that misled and made you double back in anger.
They might erase the trail completely with leaves,
go away one morning without any thanks or explanations.
Go after them: dig for their traces under the loam of woods.
When you are out there in the woods behind the house,
if your grandmother calls you to come home again,
don't answer her, don't go back!

The Grandmother

She liked her own relations best,
the formality of albums
and well-dressed, well-appointed ways.

Her world of Cincinnati
slept inside itself like a book —
the red leatherbound engagement book
on its hook above the hall table.

What of the dead beyond the churchyard wall,
blooming yellow-red in autumn
with its cover of leaves and bittersweet berries?

The dead have no albums, no engagement books.
Only the dry leaves for cover —
the shuttle-fall of leaves and the locusts' bright cases,
strewn over the playground grass in summer.

Ghosts of a Battleground

The mountain men came from behind trees
as the sun was setting.
They had snakeskin belts,
fringed leggings and moccasins, like the Indian.
Their moccasins knew grass,
as if they had been shadows.

When my ancestor stepped into the clearing,
he heard the quick sighing of an arrow.
The Indian stopped and turned towards him,
arms spotted like deer by the light
through a thick canopy of leaves.

He stood there for a moment like a messenger,
then disappeared into the trees.

Then James Laird began to remember
who he was.   He was the heat of the sun,
the red lance of daylight behind cold marshes.
He was the heron who flies out of sight
along the last line of trees before dark.

The Wind at Evening

lifts the light charcoal of leaves.
Things soften and declare themselves:
the dance of dust along a windowsill,
slow beckoning of trees.

Lifting the mask of leaves away
at twilight, along the housefronts.
Where I sit by the yellow-brown, orchard wall,
chickadees begin a song against growing dark —
in the wind's pauses.

Views of Pompeii

Comings and goings through a windy house. Girls,
we were in costumes then from hid to fort.   Grandmother
made us, on her Soaring-machine.   You were the Queen, I was
Lady-in-Wailing.   Grandmother made us, then she put us up
to bid.

.She kept strict track of the birds, Grainmother did.
Hung pots of suet in window trays.   And in soft, matchable
dresses and shoes, weekend gusts went in and out.   I was sad,
I was scalded, because I put on a too-long dress with a
violent sash.

Grandmother scolded me, for weeping such a lawn
time.   Was it sobbishness?   I cried a bit, until they said I
would get pinkeye.   She was cutting out new cloths on her
Soaring-machine.   Why pink on me?

They stared at us, her soft windowblind of friends.   Sent
us their blank looks, their views of Pompeii and Niagara,
weekend presence and the fine linen of their thank-you-nots.

Grandmother, we were in hiding then, your dress-alike
twins, your new moths. We played house, or stayed hid
in our crises, bundled up on limbs of the tall, Hand-me-down
apple trees.

The Night before Christmas

It was tea-time in Effortless Hall. The throngbirds had opened their throats. It was Teaterm. It was tantrum. The pessimism trees were increasing sourness, all our acorns had aches. Rhododendrons said long, sad words about themselves, weeping like rainbuckets.

Then a fearful racket arose. It was Sister at the piano, playing up a storm in the green-ivied Moratorium. While tree-toads had their visions. We gazed through the Scary-o-scope, at Marines in blue Victory gardens. Life was a war, it was wary, when we were only three.

Mother was not at home. She and Stoutfellow, her true-horse, skyed and scarumed out over the windytops. On Dashing, on Dancing, she fled like a Comet! Things were going from bad to worse, in Mother's amusing mansion.

While bees held their matinees, the chimneyswifts had naps, and Japanese beetles went on bombing the daylights out of the ripe, Oriental cherry trees.

The Moon

begins to climb over fences,

the barn with its wide door and hayloft

and the creaking, rustling of forgotten things.

A trapdoor in the hayloft leads off into nothingness.

The white moon like a mother steps across into the darkness.

She looks for her children over the barn's wide, shadowed floor.

An upturned wheelbarrow leans in the corner, half-caked with dirt.

Bags of lime, of cement. A hayrake stands upright against the wall.

The moon leans for a moment against the barn's wide, half-open door

and learns many things: her eye can detect mice or set long poles

quivering in the shadows. Now the moon begins to climb up over

the white barn with trapdoor and ladder. She looks at the

scarcely breathing hill. Not thinking of itself at all.

She looks for her children over the wide, white world

that is almost without shadows now.

Not thinking of itself

at all.

Babar

1. In the City

Babar came to live in the city, far from Cornelius and all
the elephants.   Here everything was laid out in rows; the
flowers grew in formal plots.   His only friend was the Old
Lady, who took him for walks in the Park and bought him a
new green suit.   She took him for his first elevator ride, high
onto a terrace where pigeons roosted on windows of the
elephant buildings.   The lobbies were made of grillwork,
like the gold lace on Cornelius's black hat.

Babar grew ill with a fever and was afraid to sleep.   His
new green suit was the color of nightmares that walk on air
and have wrinkled foreheads.   The Old Lady paraded
mysteriously at night in the hallway, but soothed his fever,
brought him medicine in a spoon.   Once, because he cried
for a long-lost whiteness, for his father shot by gamekeepers,
she came and sat for a long time at the edge of the bed,
smoothed the covers and told him stories, while the city
roared at them from a distance.

When the fever went away, they sat in two armchairs in
front of the fire, while the maid brought them tea on a round
tray, with thin bread and butter.   The Old Lady showed him
photographs, smoothed out the pinkish, faded edges and
spoke of her mother, and the brother who rode away to war.

He watched the ink well up in the inkwell when she filled it, listened to her voice with its strong views, sudden laughter and playfulness.

She took him into her high, climactic house, as into a book whose chapters were bathed in love, a kind of wisdom. She taught him to respect himself, to insist on what was highly-colored, instinctive. Would it also be his duty to fly from what was dull and dishonest, like a sickroom dream?

2. In the Country

In the morning she sat at her desk, opening its many small drawers and cubbyholes. She showed him how to heat and soften the bars of sealingwax, to seal long white envelopes. A watch in a blue enamelled case hung from her shoulder, and she let him examine it: the small, precise numerals were in blue, her color.

There were times when she seemed to go away from him; her sitting-room door would be closed, and he'd be told to amuse himself quietly in the garden. When he was welcomed back, they exclaimed together over a volume of old prints. She showed him a painting of a city on a hill. In the foreground, a woman was kneeling; perhaps she had come there to pick flowers, or had just combed her hair, into waves so small and exact it was almost a sound, like the plucking of a harp.

Then Babar had a fever again, and was put to bed in a high, quiet room at the back of the house. Here voices came and went, from a world that was never solid. In dreams he saw monsters of sea-green, their heads turned around backwards, on which other monsters rode bareback. He thought often of the Old Lady, but when she came in to look at him, he was not sure she had really been there. Others came carrying something to eat on a tray; he could only open his eyes, look, and close them again; and they went away, shaking their heads.

When he was recovering he lay on a couch by the open window. The smell of early morning reminded him of church: the hymnals neatly stacked in red covers, all in freshest, clearest print. Other smells came back to him — the smell of bicycles in the rain; the smell of the third grade schoolroom (this was a complex smell of cookies, fresh milk and fingerpaint).

He still grew tired easily, and would sit for hours in an armchair, while Delia polished the silver nearby. Or he watched the dressmaker, or the woman who came to trim hats.

At last the day came when he was pronounced well enough to go for a drive. The car waited at the door, motor humming. There was Delia hurrying back and forth to find a handkerchief or a lost pair of spectacles. There was John standing to attention by the running board, the grey carriage robe folded neatly over his arm. The car, deeply polished as a mirror, slid forth among hydrangeas still wet from rain, shedding blossomcups over the black, polished hood. John stared back at them through the round eye of the rear-view mirror, his own eye large and expressionless.

For My Grandmother

ELLEN FARNSWORTH LOOMIS

In the house, there was always water falling,
inside or outside, in candlelight, sun, or shade,
in late years, when there were few visitors.

To climb up beside you as a child on the sofa,
bearing some book from your desk or library.
So carefully opening the dark things with a letterknife
not to harm them.   The released pages flew up like hands
in the quiet of the lamp-shadowed room.

Your sons left you in a garden.
You smiled, sitting in an old, tilt-back chair
towards evening, to talk to visitors.
They were looking at the things of your life.

Your helplessness seemed more real
than the efficiency of others.
Able to be alone, to be kind,
while others cared for the universe,
you kept the inward gravity of your view.

If there is anywhere else for you,
may it have your innocent lightness.
May it be like a great house, doors opened wide,
the curtains drawn, the linen laid out,
and the candles all lit, preparing for children.

VOICES

The River

I need room, says the river, for rustling,
for the passages of wind and wintry sun.
In spring, I need crawling along boughs,
the wakefulness of insect and tadpole
as each falls into my shadow.   In the woods,
in deep depressions of the wind and dampest ground,
I find my pure notes: nests of violets,
the Indianpipes crouching on thin legs.
In autumn I need rest, I need bird-strength.
The knowledge rises in me of a journey
to an unknown place, whose paths keep whispering
and closing behind me to the forest's rim.
The way each leaf is shed, each fiery vowel
nods downward from a tree-limb.

The Rain

When I awoke, it was in sunlight.
Soft words were spoken nearby; in the distance
a schoolbell chimed.   I had such messages!
I wanted to roll out over hillsides,
speak into rivers . . .

To have walked over the wide earth,
a pilgrim, knocking softly at your door,
kneeling at the thresholds.   Waking,
to descend into the twilight . . .

O Sister, I cannot tell you enough
in this one time of falling,

this hurrying forest,
the wakeful silence that is myself.

For Ishi

Turtle thought he had made the world up
in the sleep of the old days.
He had thought it out
in his small head perfectly mounted,
eyes that missed nothing.

Turtle was growing out of a soft rock.
He put forth his head strangely,
as if the shell yawned and threw out its legs.

He had pulled the world from the dark mirrors of his shell,
from a dark smoke-hole in the middle of himself.

First he painted the sky,
finished it with a bone scraper.
Then he stretched out the roofing of the night,
and covered it with moisture of starlight.

Now, as if falling asleep, he kept closing his eyes.
He held the lids perfectly shut.

Turtle thought he had made the world up,
chipping and chipping with an old bone chisel.
He reminds me of my sister,
of our tent-village, pitched on a narrow ledge
above the Deer Creek river.

Ishi was the Indian, the last of his tribe, who appeared in Oroville,
California in 1911. His people had hidden themselves for fifteen years in
the foothills above the town. He was befriended by the anthropologist A.
Kroeber, who took him to live in the Anthropological Museum at Berkeley.

Elm Trees

They look like elephants.   Their falling leaves are strewn from elephants' howdahs.   Small birds peck around the feet of the elephants, and they are rocking, the elephants, from side to side, shifting the great work of holding the universe.

At evening everything turns: the earth, the leaves around the base of the huge, wind-shadowed trees.   Winter turns toward us like a fan its dark, unpainted side.   Stars grow like frost.   A teaching silence stirs, like bark over the tall trees.   Thick bark over the names of this world.

Inside Mahler's Songs Again

A space widens out,
the sense of insecurity, of darkness,
and the security of which old, dark carriages are made:
creaking, anonymous noises, the width and promise
of the velvet seats.   Like sitting in an old, abandoned carriage
in the barn, in the rain.   Driving through night,
the coachmen's faces are the distant night-faces of children
turned into the wind, blurred and a little heavy,
like the faces of people who ride all night in trains.

Their eyes are open, and look out
to the wide midnight, and the lowing of fields.
In this poem of the strange darkness of which old carriages
     are made,
you had to get used to the emptiness and waiting in little
     streets,
used-up cafés on the outskirts of cities.   You had to die a little.

The night keeps on pouring you out, and takes everything in;
feeding the air, the dark cornfields on the edges of the
     knowledge of death,
the angels with pointed wings, and their questionings of light,
and the dawn, and the journey.   Night yawns and takes
     everything in.

Permanence

Earth turning round with us in the night,
stitching us into the sky.

All the places we have been to
Earth gives back to us in whispers.
The rain falls low from a roof;
your voice travels on,
threading through the night.

I begin to believe we might be happy.
The sky that loves us wraps us round —
sky lovers in a quilt of rich design,
or an old story.

Nightwatch

Listen to what happened in the night. When I looked to
see if it was daylight, my heart seemed stiff. The room was
cold, as if turning to go. What if I loved you? If you could
see me facing you in that place lovers go to, walking over the
unknown grass, walking about under the trees. You know,
its breeze is unexplained. If you could see me, feel the
breeze coming through windows of the salt-white houses,
gently turning back curtains. Where lovers are beginning to
awaken, to turn towards windows and say to one another:
"Listen to what happened in the night."

The Salmon

They were painted by the Old Masters:
lapis lazuli against a background of white;
along the spine, yellow-green of malachite.

They are helmeted saints, rising up
to a moment in early spring:
robes fan backwards, air flames away
from the moment, the tremor that is in air.

Like a tongue which never varies,
speaking the same truth year after year —
a whole city of tongues . . .

When they leap into the spray,
they become angels, the grim-visaged saints,
and the rainbows that played backwards from them.

A Life

She came spinning down
towards the Earth.

She came spinning like a cloth coat
into the nighttime traffic —
next to a Park.

Sometimes a life, steadily looked at,
is unbearable.   Too much is expected —
too little known.

What does the other, the grandmother, say
of her granddaughter's plunge and passage,
sitting high in a room in the glass penthouse?

"It isn't death that counts.   It's the things
life does to you that matter."

The other falls, and seems to linger.
Her body eats into the placid air
above the nighttime city, beside the Park.

All that moves is difficult
to hold in view — all love,
and the numbness of grieving.
Next passage: the unmoving dark.

Milkweed

When it bursts, the seeds
ascend along trails in the sunlight,
through woods and around tree-trunks,
like prisoners released into the sun.
They will remove and wash their white shirts
in cold rivers, before they rise again.

This Year

The high wind of your distractions
has blown down our good house.
It was gone as suddenly as it came.

Now there are doors and windows
left standing on a hilltop.

What will I do when summer comes?
No warm wooden porches to ponder the heat.
Only doors open onto a faceless dark.

What will I do when summer
lifts the ladle of its waters
to fill all the summer fields with ponds?

Will the brown log be broken
where we stepped across one day —
spring air darkened by the leaves overhead,
other leaves the wind had swept under
darkening, brimming the crystal water.

Chinese Calligraphy

Was it the tigers who invented the characters?
Tigers twisting and untwisting their tails to make new
meaning.   When a tiger came towards me, I could stroke
him, his hide felt like velvet.   That was how I learned
the way the land approaches and vanishes, leaving a
silence of water, which is the tiger's footprints.

Rorschach Test

There is a kingdom whose contours are receding,
baffling the experts, who keep on sending
boatloads of observers up the Congo River
in paddlewheelers and tophats
to observe the insidious event.

There is an international come-as-you-are party
on board an unidentified ocean liner,
where scientists escaped from inkbottles
are squirting ink over unsuspecting passengers;
while ship's detectives, following some robbers,
bump into one another on the revolving dancefloor,
and a tall, first-class passenger in false whiskers
sits by the railing, innocently eating squid.

The Lily

FOR CAROLINE

Light goes, is drawn by, and divides,
the lily speaks through the length of the quiet room.
It mingles light earth-talk with laughter again,
into each room it comes and goes, speaks softly with you.

Somewhere light is a gift, somewhere it is cherishing us.
The light goes, is drawn by, and divides,
and somewhere the lily is speaking,
through the length of the room, through the quiet afternoon.

Into each room it comes, hastening with you;
into each corner it goes, hides softly with eyes.
The lily makes whole again, brushes the silence and goes
hastening with you, among green shadows.

Nijinsky

This burning, this fluttering —
hundreds of mothwings
under the worn footlights —
has made me afraid.

They said: Explain to us
how you are suffering.
Explain meant, put an end
to this wandering in snow,
the soft, white-lit miracle:
explain meant a curtain.

I came into these mountains
looking for my miracles.
Each day I climb their stiff, unbending sides
unfettered by storm or winds.
I run on like a leaf, not stopping —
at night I fall like a stone.

Once, stepping back from the brink
of some dull cliff, I saw Diaghilev —
a dark, admonishing hand
raised in the whirling whiteness.

Each night now, that dark bird
that will devour my life
sits down on the horizon,
waiting, sharpening its claws.

Book of Hours

At first, from quaking underfoot, came irises and leaves,
half-hidden beside a path.   From the rustling grass came
      sparrows,
the ducking head, grasp of a foot from the sibilant grass,
the murmur of leaves.   From the ground, from the margins
came mountain lion, pheasant, the phoenix with outstretched
      wing.

They wanted to lift the land of our breathing
in their teeth and bright beaks, like a canopy
high into the trees, in the breathing of squirrels,
with their breathing-in-and-out among branches,
half-opened leaves of the chestnut and the linden.

The people were still folded inside of letters,
inside of life sleeping soundly, as in a tree.
First a shoulder, then an arm undid itself
from the trunk of a letter.   Small figures hurried out,
each carrying a stone, to add to the path, beside the path,
which was also a ladder, crisscrossing the light of rivers.

From the twining of the boughs
came dragons with human heads, round O's of knowledge,
the Q standing high in the stirrups.   The shape of the letter L
was filled with music, with angels on lutes and the watching
      of lions.
All this happened quietly, mortally, from the beginning,
the first tender appearance of the leaves.

Voices

Last night I heard powerful voices
reaching and stirring, finding headlong a rescue,
to forge through an outlet into sea-light.

In the calling of dreams I see myself ahead,
in the opening of rooms where I have not yet been —
but I have been there.   I remember the song-rooms,
green-reflected to the ceiling, stirred by the tides
and open to sea-light.   I have caught reflections
of the men and women who entered before me.

In the opinion of walls there is nothing.
In the opinion of rooms where I am there *is*
no opening.   Breathe me a tunnel,
break through the wall, this thing, this nothing
and be a rescue.   Break through for me
into song-light, even in dreams.

The Market
of Zagreb:
A Winter Calendar

OCTOBER   The drivers unload their wagons.   Bundles of lettuce descend from frosted wagonbeds.   The horses stamp their hooves and know winter is coming; they can smell the scent of apples in the baskets brought to market, feel the skin of light drawn more tightly, finely over the bones of these days.

It is early morning.   A heart made of bread and glass hangs in a shopwindow.   In another window are the small cooking utensils carved out of wood: spoons, breadboards, miniature rollingpins.   If the children wanted a banquet to unite all people, if they baked for a week, could they use all the implements in this one, narrow window?

Now cold settles into the branches of the trees, and in the nostrils of the horses.   The horses' necks are bent with fatigue, as they lean into the lamplight.   They can hear the swift music of the footsteps along cobblestones.   They can smell darkness, feel the distance they have come, along invisible roads before dawn.

The name of each separate thing grows under the tongue, the way it grows in the land. As I enter the market, words sound brusque: "luk" is the word for onion, "marelica" means apricot. What is the different, dream name for these things?

NOVEMBER   It is two months since I came to Zagreb to study singing, to stay with my teacher and his wife in their apartment on Preradović Street.   Each morning I go to market, past the cobbler's shop on the corner, the war veteran in his wheelchair by the entrance to the marketplace. I climb stone steps worn smooth at the center, where women with red and blue shopping nets come to catch morning, like a fish from the fish seller's marble basin.   One woman owns a flower; another tosses carrots and greenery into her net. They fill the air with arguments, calling "Gospodja!" or "Gospodiča!" which means "Madame" or "Miss."   Now the government frowns on these old-fashioned titles.   The new world wants to say "Careful!" to everyone.

Independence Day
November 29

The whole population is out today, in red kerchiefs, wool hats and blue workers' uniforms. Some go to church, some peddle their wares, or stroll through the stalls of the open market. Pigeons tumble under the tables, picking up seeds or the dry favors of bread.

The mushrooms rise early. They are the envy of everyone — leeks, onions, fiery tomatoes. They bring them in in truckloads: the mushroom is on the march! Black birds fly up from glistening tables; the sky darkens — a sea of birds! Mushrooms die bravely, on parades or in mushroom salads.

The peppers are coming to town, leaping in their red and green uniforms. They are turning towards us in the sun; they want to bombard everybody! Church steeples are in green, announcing the new day.

How does it feel to be an apple, to hang in the warm sun, be brought to market in an openwork basket lined with straw, along with leeks, turnips, the hill-shaped levels of eggs?

DECEMBER   The noonday cannon sounds from the walls of the Old Town overhead, causing pigeons to take off in their wide arcs over the rooftops.   The snow voice of the air grows keener; the pigeons know it; they circle up and up, reach plum-high steeples, the balconies in the Old Town facing towards forests — the snow-mountain Slijeme, and the Austrian hunting lodge with its black, mirror lake.

What are they saying, the old brown women, the onion women of the market with their heads wrapped in shawls, brushing flies from their wares?   Their language is the rubbing together of branches, in the countryside where birds fly down into bundles of dried stalks.   Where the old man yokes oxen to a cart, sets out in early morning to go to market.   The old woman listens, a gold straw between her teeth.

Birds have given up their wings.   They know a bird seller will come, to take them to the tall city, still sleeping in December light.   The old man hauls a load of brushwood up the hill by the frozen lake.   The weather shines gold in all the margins.

JANUARY   In my lesson in the afternoon we work on the Mahler songs — about the dead soldier who returns, and the child who waits for the reward of bread, of sympathy, that will never come.   It is getting late, but my teacher has not turned on the lights.   We try over the line that begins "How long have you been standing."   It is low in the middle range and very quiet, very difficult to sing.

He shows me a book called *The Psychology of the Vibrato*. What we hear as a single note may be a series of sounds of different intensities.   The unevenness is a part of all good singing, deeply rooted in the emotions.

I can now call on deeper resources in my body, but not always, and not right away.   Sometimes for no reason things work out well for me: the telephone rings, or Dara flings open the door to the studio.   Afterwards it is easier to release the breath, and the song takes on a life of its own.

Crossing the wide playing-field after dark I hear them talking. Language is a wind-machine made out of bits of glass, bits of colored cloth and metal. It is full of movement like a tree, or the dance of the 297 bones of the human body. "Razgovor" is a word that seems made for the forests: dark pinetrees, lofty cedars; but the word means only "talk."

FEBRUARY   The farmers have been coming in for hours, bringing flowers, vegetables and fruit for the open market. The farmers' faces look brown and mended, like cloth that has been turned and re-used many times. Someone tells me the farmers are getting rich now, while the government sets prices, that many own their own warehouses in town.

The peasants live where cornsheaves rustle, in solid white houses of two or more floors, with room underneath for the animals: sometimes a bullock, some chickens or a goat. They bake ornamental bread for the holidays. They live like the rest of us, fear the bringing of yellow flowers, which means death.

Šestina Village

Down the village street, a woman brings oxen home
from the fields. Birds fly and perch on the farmyard wall.
The smoke disappears down a chimney.
    The piled branches in the farmyard wait for the farmer's
axe to split them, for the dying sun to light them to a blaze,
that will spread over fields, where new corn is rustling . . .

That old woman was a horse-chestnut tree once . . .

The field that was an owl brings good advice in the
winds of the evening, beneath a cypress hill. Now, from a
nest under the earth, darkness rises. The houses disappear,
are led away one by one like oxen. To lie down until morning
in the aromas of hay, the stone clinking of harness.

MARCH   It is nearly Easter.   In the Russian Orthodox Church on the corner they are selling Easter cards; soon the finely decorated eggs will appear.   Today Katitsa the maid will not be here; she has gone with her son to visit the vineyard they own outside the city, where they must plant a certain kind of grass to prevent weeds from growing.   This morning she left a pot of meat wrapped in cabbage leaves on the stove for us.

In the flower market it is still early; the farm women are setting plants out on tables, separating the roots, placing cut flowers in tin tubs.   I walk along between tables, comparing the different plants and their prices.   The women in heavy sweaters and woolen shawls call out to me in harsh, heavily underlined voices.

Each flower is a softly breathing flame hidden among leaves.   The name of each is like a cool, dark spirit: "ruža," "tulipan," "zumbul," "cyklamé . . ."

Sabra Loomis was born in Cincinnati, grew up in Virginia and New York and graduated from Radcliffe College in 1960. For a long time she travelled, gave concerts and studied singing. She is a concert singer who has lived in many cities, including Boston, New York, Paris, and Zagreb. While living in Yugoslavia, she began to write the poems collected in this book. In 1989 she received an MA from the graduate Creative Writing program at N.Y.U. This is her first full-length book of poems.

POETRY FROM ALICE JAMES BOOKS